What Our Readers Have Said...

"Although I consider myself a seasoned sales professional, it is helpful to have past learning's refreshed. The books were also beneficial because of the information concerning 'trends' in the sales relationship. The sales process should be viewed as dynamic since business relationships change regularly."

•

"For the particular business I am in and the type of sales calls I have, I find that the books in the Pinpoint Sales Training Series are very often applicable to how I conduct business. I would recommend them to other sales people, just not ones that are in my industry."

•

"These books provide very good concepts. It fits in well with the Bell Leadership training program that I attended in November."

•

"I use this material in these books and apply it to my customers and other employees I work with."

•

"I would like to know other topics. Is there anything on Production Management or Consultative Selling or Time Management?"

•

"These books are great tools that should be used as guidelines for our everyday

supervisory practices. You need to take the time to do a short self-evaluation when reading them."

•

"The Pinpoint Training Series delivers information that could be used in a lot different areas."

•

"I like this because I can take them with me to read at a convenient time. I feel the little time I have to spend in the office is best use on activities that directly relate to revenue opportunities. I like the short amount of time it takes to keep up with these."

•

"I prefer the self-study approach; it fits in with my schedule."

•

"My thought is that the real value of these books comes into effect when doing the action plans."

•

"Short and sweet. These books are easy to comprehend."

•

"I have enjoyed reading these books. They are relevant to today's work environment and the ongoing change in the way we manage our workforce."

•

"I do feel that these books have been very helpful to me at my job."

•

"I think a lot of the recommendations in these books are very useful, and can be applicable to everyday situations. If nothing else, it's a good reference guide to fall back upon if a situation arises in the future."

•

"These books are relevant to today's work environment and the ongoing change in the way we manage our workforce."

•

Productive Qualifying Strategies

Pinpoint Sales Skill Development Training Series

TIMOTHY F. BEDNARZ

MAJORIUM
BUSINESS PRESS

Pinpoint Sales Skill Development Training Series
"Productive Qualifying Strategies"
Timothy F. Bednarz

Graphic design: Monika Pawlak

Majorium Business Press
2025 Main Street
Stevens Point, WI 54481
715.342.1018 • 800.654.4935

ISBN 978-1-882181-82-7

Printed in the United States of America

Introduction

The Pinpoint Sales Skill Development Training Series is designed for targeted training and education regarding increased improvement in a specific skill or competency.

Each book within this series is designed to be easy to use, understand and apply to your job. It can be used as a basis for training individuals, as a discussion guide or as a personal training tool.

Each chapter within this book discusses a specific concept. When you have completed all eight chapters you should have a 360° perspective of the topic.

Additionally, each chapter is divided into specific sections:

- The first section provides you with an overview of the topic
- The Implications section discusses why the concept is important, and why it is important to learn and apply.
- The Strategies, Tips & Techniques to Apply section teaches how to use and apply the particular concept to your work.
- The Points to Ponder section gives you something to think about or to be discussed with a group setting. These are questions not meant to be immediately answered, but to be pondered over time.
- The Training Activity section provides you with the tools to transfer what you have learned to your job. It is designed to help create an action plan to effectively apply the concept.

Each of the topics in this series is time-tested and proven in the marketplace. They have been used by thousands of employees as training tools. Many of the users have commented that what made these books valuable, was the ability to refer to them when a problem surfaced. They indicated that they remembered reading about the exact problem. They referred back to these books and found an appropriate solution.

You will find them equally valuable as a resource in your professional development library.

Table of Contents

LEARNING OBJECTIVES:

- To understand the importance of qualifying.
- To identify the consequences of failing to qualify.
- To analyze how to qualify a prospect.
- To determine how to properly qualify a prospect.
- To know if and when a prospect is properly qualified.
- To uncover hidden needs and opportunities.

1

Understanding the Concept of Qualifying

Objections, sales stalls and sales barriers are generally caused by the direct actions of the salesperson. The roots of any objection are found in the qualification process at the beginning of the sale. This is where and when the salesperson should be collecting and probing for information.

IMPLICATIONS — WHAT THIS MEANS TO YOU

Salespeople cannot shorten the qualification phase without experiencing objections and resistance later in the sale. The salesperson who effectively gathers the essential information and develops the necessary tools to diagnose the problem is able to craft an impressive and workable sales solution.

Salespeople can take the time to develop and analyze information—or they can spend their time fighting objections. They will be perceived as more professional by gathering and diagnosing rather than dealing with the conflict objections bring to the sales relationship.

There are no shortcuts in selling. The salesperson who attempts to short-circuit the process is only creating more headaches for him or herself.

STRATEGIES, TIPS & TECHNIQUES TO APPLY

Many objections occur because the salesperson has failed to gather the specific information needed to develop a unique and credible solution or because they have failed to educate the customer about their unique offer.

Proper qualifying of a prospect goes beyond establishing a need for a particular product or service. There are a number of other factors that must be considered before the salesperson can move the process forward:

Financial Considerations

A primary consideration that should be immediately focused upon is the prospect's financial ability to purchase the product or service. During economic slowdowns, the salesperson must also determine whether the prospective purchase is budgeted for and if so, when the monies will be available. In business downturns, many companies can afford to make a purchase, but may choose not to make any new and major financial commitments until conditions improve. As the economy improves, this caution may remain until complete confidence is restored.

A prospect's ability to afford a product or service is often a sensitive issue. The prospect may consider their financial information confidential, or they may fear they will be charged more than they are prepared to pay once this information is revealed.

Salespeople need to probe for a financial range that is within the limits of what the prospect is prepared to spend for the product or service. This provides the necessary input needed to craft a solution that comes within the proper parameters.

Determine Decision Makers

The second primary factor a salesperson needs to identify is a list of all of the decision makers involved in the buying decision. Selling to a person who lacks purchasing authority only wastes the salesperson's time and resources. Purchasing committees make most major buying decisions. Salespeople need to identify all of the committee members, as well as their authority and responsibilities.

Purchasing Time Frame

The third primary factor salespeople need to determine is the purchasing time frame the prospect will be following. Sales are often lost due to poor timing. Many prospects may be laying the groundwork for future purchases, but delaying a final decision until the economy improves. Salespeople need to determine when the prospect plans to make the purchase and plan their sales strategy accordingly. However, due to the volatility of the economy, it may be productive to work with a prospect who is laying the groundwork for a future purchase. A sudden upturn can quickly lead to a buying decision.

As the salesperson qualifies a prospect, he or she needs to uncover the competitive situation and identify what if any other products the prospect is considering. A competitive comparison of these products will help the salesperson position him or herself with the prospect and verify their budget ranges.

Eliminate Objections

The final stage of qualifying a prospect involves eliminating as many objections as possible by asking questions and soliciting feedback. Salespeople should think ahead and consider the most common objections they may encounter throughout the qualifying process. Proper qualification eliminates most objections by identifying specific needs and developing solutions based upon the information provided by the prospect.

Shortest Path to a Sale

Properly done, qualifying establishes a salesperson's professionalism and creates a firm foundation upon which to build future sales. Salespeople who properly identify and pre-qualify prospects by conducting a structured prospecting search will have developed sufficient information to make their qualification call a productive undertaking with few or no surprises. Thorough research enables salespeople to quickly identify the prospect's hidden needs, agendas and pressing issues. They will know exactly where to focus their questions and efforts.

While it may appear to take more time than most salespeople wish to invest in a sale, it is firmly established that a well-prepared approach to qualifying a prospect is the shortest path to building sales and developing relationships.

POINTS TO PONDER — SOMETHING TO THINK ABOUT

1. What additional factors do you feel you need to consider when qualifying a prospect?
2. What problems and pitfalls have you encountered by not adequately qualifying a prospect? Explain.

TRAINING ACTIVITY — APPLICATION & ACTION PLAN

1. Outline on a sheet a paper, the steps you take and the information you collect when you qualify a prospect.
2. Compare your qualification process against the strategies listed above and identify any gaps.
3. Develop a qualifying checklist that you can use with future prospects.

2

The Implications of Qualifying

Salespeople often make assumptions about a prospect based upon their previous experience and expertise. The assumptions that they make have implications that can bias the entire sale and result in unnecessary objections and stalls that can cause future problems and concerns.

IMPLICATIONS — WHAT THIS MEANS TO YOU

Quality selling techniques stems directly from the salesperson's need for information. Without accurate facts and data, salespeople are unable to adequately address a prospect's needs with a unique solution. Their sales habits become sloppy and rather than take the time to properly qualify a new prospect, they assume because the circumstances appear to be similar, the facts will remain the same. This results is specific ramifications and implications during the sale

This is important for salespeople to understand since each prospect is unique with their own set of needs, wants, problems and concerns. Undoubtedly salespeople will see commonality and automatically assume they know what the prospect needs. While the solution might often be the same, each has to be addressed on its own merits.

STRATEGIES, TIPS & TECHNIQUES TO APPLY

The need to qualify prospects is unquestionable, but there are implications that salespeople need to be aware of including:

Need

The prospect's need for a product or service is a fundamental factor that must be explored before a salesperson begins to sell. Salespeople cannot assume there is a need or even the extent of the need. Yet it is surprising how many salespeople completely skip over this fact and automatically assume there is a need when one has not be established. Similar companies might use a specific product or service, but just because one uses it and finds it useful does not mean another has a similar perspective.

Affordability

The second most fundamental factor before a sale can be made is the prospect's ability to afford the product. Recent economic conditions have had many companies tightening their belts and looking closely at every single expenditure. In this light, affordability takes on a new perspective. Even if a company in the past has purchased a product or service, they might now view similar purchases differently. They might think that specific purchases are now a luxury or are not in their budget.

Salespeople cannot assume that a company can automatically afford a product or that it's an item that is automatically budgeted for. It is likely this will remain an issue in the marketplace until companies are comfortable with economic conditions.

Timing

The timing of a sale or when an order is to be placed certainly affects the outcome of a sale. It is not safe for a salesperson to assume that a sale is automatically going to be placed at the conclusion of the sales process.

Most companies will budget their expenditures during the year and these can be impacted both, positively or negatively, by their sales and demand for their product. This is a specific factor that salespeople cannot make assumptions about. In certain instances during the recent economic turndown, budgets were slashed and schedules revised as the economy quickly soured. This rapidly changed sales conditions and impacted the sales opportunities for many salespeople.

Authority

Many salespeople assume that the person making an inquiry, eliciting information and discussing their product or service has the automatic authority to approve the purchase. In fact, as companies move toward the use of buying groups and committees, buying authority is often diffused over several individuals. Salespeople must clarify who has the purchasing authority and how specific decisions are arrived at.

Often when assumptions about authority are made and when the buyer makes no efforts to change the perception that he or she is in charge, problems can arise when the time arrives to make a decision. Embarrassment over this issue often results in stalls and objections.

Unique Solutions

In certain instances salespeople will attempt to sell what they want to sell rather than what the prospect wants or needs. Assumptions that are made based on previous experiences are faulty. Even when similar companies are being sold to, each will have individual problems, concerns and issues that must be addressed on their own merits. Salespeople cannot assume that the same solution always fits varying needs. Even if they do, they must be presented in a manner that addresses the prospect's individual wants, needs, problems and concerns.

POINTS TO PONDER — SOMETHING TO THINK ABOUT

1. Have you ever been caught off-guard by making assumptions about a prospect that proved to be untrue? Explain.
2. Have you lost sales due to faulty assumptions? Explain.

TRAINING ACTIVITY — APPLICATION & ACTION PLAN

1. Take the time to review all of the assumptions you typically make when meeting with a prospect.
2. List on a sheet of paper these assumption and next to each the basis of the assumption.
3. Determine the validity of each and whether you should be making them.

3

Factors That Impact Qualifying a Sale

Salespeople have an obligation to sell a prospect if a need exists and he or she has the ability to make a purchase. Often salespeople feel that once they have established those two facts, their responsibility to further qualify the prospect concludes. However qualifying a prospect entails a number of other factors that ultimately impact the salesperson's success or failure with the prospect.

IMPLICATIONS — WHAT THIS MEANS TO YOU

Unless the salesperson is selling a relatively simple item, more sales are becoming increasingly more complex. Buying decisions that were once made by a single decision maker are now the responsibility of a buying committee. An increase of buying channels and product options have made product evaluation more time consuming and complicated. Buyers are better trained and more sophisticated. Consequently, the sale of a product or service can consume a great deal of a salesperson's time and resources.

This is important because salespeople are not paid to sell but to generate sales and revenue. In this regard, qualifying becomes an aspect of time and resource management. When salespeople properly qualify a prospect, they are identifying where to invest their resources to obtain the best results. Salespeople are assessing where they can get the best return on their investment.

STRATEGIES, TIPS & TECHNIQUES TO APPLY

Salespeople are the facilitators of change. The process of selling involves convincing prospects to make changes in their business that can have an impact on their business. An essential part of selling, establishing rapport and building trust is reducing the level of risk in the prospect's mind to minimize his or her resistance to change. Consequently, the higher the levels of perceived risk and resistance to change, the longer the entire sales process will take.

As a time and resource management issue salespeople must be cognizant of these factors. Since they are often under pressure to produce results, they must balance their time and resources between the prospects that have relatively low resistance to change and those with high levels who may take longer to fully develop to the point of commitment. Typically, larger and more lucrative prospects may fall into this category. Salespeople often create problems for themselves when they invest heavily in high resistance prospects due to the size and desirability. The heavy investment takes away from their ability to meet short-term goals and quotas.

As salespeople proceed through the qualification process, there are three factors that they must accurately assess before identifying the desirability of a prospect. These include:

Motivation

Prospects may feel that there is nothing wrong or problematic with their existing vendor. They may not be motivated to change unless the benefits far outweigh the costs associated with change. This is the specific reason that salespeople are taught to look for signs of pain or discontent with their existing suppliers. These signs identify the prospect's potential motivation to change. They have identified areas that if changed may motivate them sufficiently to make a change.

Determination

Even if motivated, a prospect may not have the will or the power to ensure that a change will occur. The political atmosphere within the company or other factors may make internal changes difficult if not impossible to make. Consequently, a lack of personal determination can result in additional resistance to change. While this can be overcome, it will take salespeople additional time and resources to facilitate internal change sufficient to reduce the risks and commit the prospect to the sale.

Willingness

The final aspect of facilitating change with a prospect is addressing whether it is worth the time and effort he or she will have to invest in changing a new product or service. Products that involve installation, training and a learning curve associated with successful implementation affect the prospect's overall motivation.

These levels of motivation can be tainted by previous bad experiences with other vendors where problems and delays occurred. Negative experiences can be associated with other similar changes and sour the prospect on the idea of even thinking about a change. These are issues that can be resolved once they are uncovered by the salesperson, but this will take additional time to reduce the risk in the prospect's mind.

Ultimately, the failure of the salesperson to identify these three qualifying factors will impact their overall results, but also provide the undercurrents that result in stalls and objections as prospects are compelled to deal with these issues as they arise.

POINTS TO PONDER — SOMETHING TO THINK ABOUT

1. Have you experienced sales situations where you thought the sale was final only to lose it for some undefined reasons?
2. Have you considered a prospect's motivation to change as you qualify him or her?

TRAINING ACTIVITY — APPLICATION & ACTION PLAN

1. Make a list of the prospects that you are currently working on.
2. Evaluate each according to their motivation, determination and wiliness to change.
3. Rate each factor on a scale of one to ten with ten being the highest.
4. Total your evaluations and prioritize your prospects according to their scores.
5. Compare and contrast this list with your own prioritized list. This should show you where to invest your time and resources first.

4

The Qualified Prospect

The time invested in properly qualifying a prospect has a strong return on investment for the salesperson who makes the effort to do so. While many attempt to short circuit the process, a properly qualified prospect is easier to sell in a shorter period of time.

IMPLICATIONS — WHAT THIS MEANS TO YOU

A properly qualified prospect should provide salespeople with the knowledge and information that they need to determine the viability of the business as a customer, the ability to determine the time and effort to sell him or her and whether a legitimate sales opportunity exists. The salesperson's goal is to identify as much of the prospect's information and criteria as possible before investing the time and resources to sell him or her.

This is important for salespeople to understand. Selling is not a game to be won or lost. It is a serious attempt to produce sales and revenues for their company. A salesperson cannot properly accomplish this task without the information to analyze and assess the prospect's business and identify their true potential as legitimate sales opportunities.

Without this information, salespeople are capable of wasting a lot of time and resources on poor sales candidates.

STRATEGIES, TIPS & TECHNIQUES TO APPLY

The following factors should be considered the basis for a qualified prospect:

Description of Problem or Need

Salespeople must be careful in defining or describing a prospect's need or problem. As simple as it seems, this is not an item that a salesperson should make assumptions about. Faulty assumptions at this stage will taint the entire sales process. Rather, salespeople should have the prospect define their own need or problem. When prospects are unable to do this, salespeople should use a series of probing questions to assist the prospect to identify his or her problems or needs. Salespeople should paraphrase and combine responses to clarify his or her problems and needs and gain agreement that this is what needs to be resolved or addressed.

Level of Discontent

The level of discontent about the existing circumstances must be clearly defined and understood by the prospect. Additionally, the salesperson must be able to engage the prospect in a meaningful two-way dialogue about key issues surrounding his or her problems. Salespeople who are unable to do this will find it difficult to sell the prospect.

Prospect's Knowledge of Solution

Prospects should have knowledge of a meaningful solution to their problems. The solution might not initially be product specific, but it should define in the prospect's mind what would be possible if not ideal.

Champions

Each change or solution needs to have individuals at senior levels to champion the change through the company. A failure to do so indicates that the seriousness of the problem is not being addressed at the appropriate levels of responsibility. Unless the salesperson identifies a champion, changes will not occur.

Motivation

The salesperson needs to identify the specific and compelling factors that are motivating the prospect to make a change and initiate the sales process. A lack of identifiable motivation can considerably lengthen the sales process.

Consequences

Prospects should be aware of the consequences associated with their choice to change or not to change their current circumstances. Salespeople should be able to quantify these into financial terms the prospect can readily understand. Additionally, salespeople should quantify the cost of opportunity lost if the prospect delays or postpones a buying decision.

Current Situation

Salespeople should have the facts and data to factually identify the prospect's current situation including the existing products or services and related costs. This allows them to develop a comparison of their solutions and costs including implementation and any associated costs to change.

Budget

Many prospects will refuse to share their budget with salespeople for several reasons:

- Fear of being taken advantage of by the salesperson.
- Lack of a budget.
- Using the salesperson to develop prices to leverage a competitor with.
- Testing the market.

Salespeople must identify the reasons for their prospect's lack of candor because each reason listed above has its own ramifications.

Alternatives

Many sales remain unresolved with no decision being made because the prospect was prepared to live with the consequences, had something else in mind or found that the risks associated with change outweighed the benefits. In other instances, prospects may have no intention of buying, using a competitor to leverage the other to get a better deal.

Evaluation

Salespeople should be aware of the criteria and standards that will be used to evaluate a product or service for selection. Additionally, they should be informed of the specific results of the evaluation and how their product or service was rated against others.

Implementation

It is a good idea for salespeople to inquire about the prospect's plans to implement a product conversion or change to determine how hare in advance he or she is thinking. This also provides insight into what and how they are thinking about the use and application of the product or service.

Expectations

Salespeople should be aware of the prospect's perceptions of what change will bring to their business and expectations of what their product or service will provide to him or her. Faulty or exaggerated expectations can result in existing and post-sale problems.

POINTS TO PONDER — SOMETHING TO THINK ABOUT

1. How extensively do you qualify your prospects? Is the process more or less intensive than described above?
2. What qualifying criteria do you feel is important for you?

TRAINING ACTIVITY — APPLICATION & ACTION PLAN

1. Examine the ramifications of each of the following reasons if a prospect refuses to disclose their budget to you.
    - Fear of being taken advantage of by the salesperson.
    - Lack of a budget.
    - Using the salesperson to develop prices to leverage a competitor with.
    - Testing the market.
2. List the possible outcomes and ramifications for each. Determine what circumstances would surround each reason and how you would identify them.

5

The Poorly Qualified Prospect

The failure to properly qualify a prospect has ramifications for the salesperson, not only by increasing sales resistance later in the sales, but ultimately in the mismanagement of time and resources. Selling should be focused primarily on producing results in the form of sales and revenues and should not become a mere exercise to fill time. Salespeople must make sure that every minute and activity is focused on moving their sales forward.

IMPLICATIONS — WHAT THIS MEANS TO YOU

Salespeople are first and foremost managers of a geographic or industrial territory for the company. In this capacity, they are responsible for the proper management of the resources allotted to them. These typically include, their time, equipment, sales resources and the financial resources budgeted to adequately perform their task. With the skyrocketing costs associated with a sales call, salespeople must make sure that the time and financial resources allotted to a prospect have a realistic expectation of a financial return for both the company and themselves.

Qualifying a prospect is an important decision making mechanism for determining where to invest limited resources for the maximum return. This is important for salespeople to understand because the salesperson who fails to properly qualify a prospect is not only shortchanging the company but also themselves.

Salespeople who fail to properly qualify a prospect and fill in the missing information with undocumented assumptions easily fall into the trap of selling and investing their time in:

The Wrong Company

As simple as it sounds, it is easy for salespeople to sell to the wrong company. On the initial level, there may be no legitimate need for a product or service. The salesperson may convince the prospect to listen to their sales presentation and invest his or her time and resources to sell a company that does not and probably will not have a need for the product or service he or she is selling.

On a deeper level, the prospect may be the wrong company due to the time and resources that must be invested to sell them. The duration of the sales process or the ultimate return on sales investment may not warrant the sales effort or may be superceded by other potential customers who offer a better potential and sales opportunity.

The Wrong Product

Salespeople can be biased toward a specific product or service they sell. This can due to past successful experiences, internal sales promotions or contests that pay a higher commission for a product sold within a specified time period.

Often salespeople will fail to identify the prospect's needs or ignore them to sell and promote a favored product. In other instances, they make a faulty assumption of the prospect's needs and identify a product or service that they feel is appropriate, but one prospect has no real interest in buying. When pushed to make a commitment, the prospect balks and throws up barriers, stalls and objections to stop the process.

The Wrong Person

An essential part of selling today is understanding the buying process within a prospective customer's company. While single individuals purchase some products, cross-functional buying teams comprised of various users, influencers and decision-makers make most buying decisions. Some have formal buying and selection procedures while others act informally. Part of the qualifying process involves identifying how buying decisions are made, who is involved and the specific procedures that are going to be followed. In this capacity the salesperson becomes a supplier of information and an influencer of the various parties associated with the final decision. The sale is not made to the initial contact person, who is often only collecting data, but to the decision-maker(s) on the buying committee.

Even when the prospect is qualified to make a buying decision, many are relying on selection and qualification committees who fulfill a similar role as the buying committee, except they may determine a selection of products or services that meet their criteria for the prospect to select from when making the final purchase.

The Wrong Time

Salespeople can expend time and resources on a prospect only to learn that the purchase was not budgeted for another six to nine months or may be pushed back to the following year's budget. In certain instances, the duration of the sales may be a natural process where the salesperson is involved in specific phases of development, influencing decisions until the final contract is awarded. However in many other situations, the time and resources are wasted until the budget for its purchase is either approved or unapproved. Often at that time, the salesperson must repeat the sales process over again, expending an equal amount of time and resources to obtain the sale.

The Wrong Budget

Salespeople can invest the time and energy to discover at the very end of the sale that the prospect does not have the budget to make the purchase, cannot gain budget approval or simply cannot afford to make the purchase. This is a circumstance that many salespeople are experiencing even as the economy is improving. Simply assuming that a company can afford a product or service is not sufficient. It is imperative that salespeople clarify with the prospect the budgetary constraints, restrictions and timetables early in the qualifying process since this may change their priority as a potential customer allowing the salesperson to focus his or her efforts elsewhere until the budget becomes available.

POINTS TO PONDER — SOMETHING TO THINK ABOUT

1. Have you viewed qualifying as a decision-making tool or as only a sales tool.
2. How do you prioritize the order that you approach and sell specific prospects?

TRAINING ACTIVITY — APPLICATION & ACTION PLAN

1. Review your recent sales performance and cite examples where you may have sold:
   - The Wrong Company
   - The Wrong Product
   - The Wrong Application
   - The Wrong Person
   - The Wrong Time
   - The Wrong Budget
2. What would you do differently?

6

The Pitfalls Associated with Qualifying

While the lack of adequately qualifying a prospect has a definite negative effect on the sale, there are a number of pitfalls that salespeople can stumble into resulting in this situation. While the lack of proper qualification is a common error salespeople make, many do so for a variety of reasons. Many are committed without the thought or understanding of the ultimate consequences. Most are committed because the importance of qualifying the prospect is minimized and downplayed in the salesperson's mind.

IMPLICATIONS – WHAT THIS MEANS TO YOU

The lack of properly qualifying a prospect is a very common among salespeople. Many do not understand its importance and do not make the connection between the problems they experience later in the sale with the lack of proper sales methodology in the initial stages. Many repeatedly encounter similar sales problems, circumstances and situations many fail to learn from their experiences because they fail to understand why they problems occur.

It is important for salespeople to understand the cause and effect of their actions or in the case of qualifying on their inaction on the entire sales process. Since each call or contact is part of the process of selling an individual prospect it does not stand-alone. Consequently, every statement and action is interrelated to all of the statements and actions taken during the sales process. Each has an impact and affects the sale. It is the sum total of the statements and actions that ultimately advances the prospect to the point of commitment. This is why what is done or left undone during qualifying a prospect has causal effects later in the sales process.

STRATEGIES, TIPS & TECHNIQUES TO APPLY

Many salespeople fail to properly qualify their prospects for a variety of reasons. While there can be many explanations, there are seven primary causes. These include:

Internal Focus

Often the internal focus of the salesperson is at the root of the problem. Many salespeople are only concerned with getting the sale. This is what drives and motivates them. Unfortunately with an internal focus, they fail to appreciate and understand the external focus needed to understand the prospect's needs and concerns. Since their motivation is purely personal, these salespeople display little care or concern about properly qualifying the prospect. If they run into problems and are unable to force their way through them, they drop the prospect and move on to other sales opportunities.

External Pressure

Often salespeople are under great pressure to perform and produce results from their sales manager and company. Their sales numbers are down or there are unable to make their quota. They are literally are under the gun to quickly produce results. In these circumstances, even when they know better, these salespeople will take short cuts in the sales process in an attempt to produce a series of quick sales. Often the results are counterproductive and the upshot is the salesperson being forced to start at the beginning to recover the sale.

Fear

Many salespeople fear asking too many questions. They are intimidated by the prospect and are fearful if they push for too much information they will irritate the prospect and lose the sale. Rather than probe and intelligently discuss the prospects need and problems so that they can craft and present a viable solution, they mentally fill in the blanks with assumptions that don't accurately describe the situation.

Assumptions

Often salespeople will sell to a number of similar companies who use similar products or services. Due to the similarities they have experienced, many salespeople have seen the same solution repeated presented and accepted. Consequently, when encountering a prospect that is similar to one that has previously been sold, assumptions are made that the same solution will apply. These salespeople don't see a need to qualify the prospect and assume they already know the situation and circumstances without offering him or her an opportunity to fully explain his or her problems and needs.

Product Bias

There are times when a salesperson is enamored with a specific product or service. The product works well, is well accepted and produces results. Consequently they have become proficient at selling it.

In these instances, these salespeople feel there is no need to qualify the prospect since, in their minds, once the prospect sees the product or service, he or she will feel the same. What are happening in these circumstances are salespeople selling what they want to sell and not what the prospect wants, needs or is even interested in.

Poor Sales Skills and Habits

Insufficiently trained salespeople develop poor sales skills and habits that are difficult to break. While sales skills can be improved, sales habits are difficult to break, so even when they are properly trained, their habits continue on. Consequently, they continue to inadequately qualify the prospect because they are comfortable with their sales methods and feel they can make any necessary corrections later on in the sales process.

Inexperience

A common cause of improper qualifying techniques is the lack of experience of the salesperson. While he or she may have attended sales training and are aware that they must qualify the prospect, he or she may not be sufficiently experienced to know and understand the depth of information they must develop. Consequently, he or she performs only a superficial qualification. When future problems are encountered, he or she is totally unaware of the connection between their failure to adequately qualify the prospect and the current stalls, objections and problems he or she is facing.

POINTS TO PONDER — SOMETHING TO THINK ABOUT

1. Are there any additional qualifying pitfalls that you may think are causing problems for you?
2. Can you think of specific situations where you may have fallen into these pitfalls? What happened and what were the results?

TRAINING ACTIVITY — APPLICATION & ACTION PLAN

1. Determine the qualifying pitfalls that you have experienced. Examine the list below and assess which situations and circumstances you have or are now experiencing.
    - Internal Focus
    - External Pressure
    - Fear

- Assumptions
- Product Bias
- Poor Sales Skills and Habits
- Inexperience

2. Identify the steps you need to take to avoid these pitfalls in the future.

7

What to Do When the Prospect Has Not Been Qualified

Since salespeople are paid to produce results in the most efficient and timely manner possible, qualifying must be a cornerstone of their efforts. Only when effective qualifying techniques are understood and applied can time and resources be prioritized and used to maximize sales effectiveness. For the salesperson just learning this distinction, what can be done with the prospects that they are already in the process of selling but may have failed to properly qualify?

IMPLICATIONS — WHAT THIS MEANS TO YOU

The salesperson who is the mist of a sale with a prospect that was not properly qualified can find himself or herself overwhelmed with problems, stalls and objections. If he or she is unaware of why this is happening, the best he or she can do is to muddle through it and hope for the best. In many situations, salespeople are trained to think this is the normal sales process and simply address one objection at a time. This follows the traditional sales track style of selling.

However, it is important for salespeople to understand that this is not the most effective method of selling. Additionally, this outmoded style of selling is based on manipulation and is being increasingly resisted by prospects. Rather than alienate the prospect, it is more effective to requalify the prospect and move forward from that point.

STRATEGIES, TIPS & TECHNIQUES TO APPLY

The following examples of symptoms as well as remedies will help the salesperson that has attempted to shortcut the prospect qualification process.

Symptoms

Inability to Move Sales Forward

Without fully understanding the prospect's wants, needs, problems and concerns there will be a sense that the salesperson and the prospect are not connecting and communication on the same levels. Since the salesperson does not have a concise understanding of what the prospect is interested in and his or her needs, the information being communicated fails to hit the mark. It is as if the both parties are speaking different languages, because in reality they are. Consequently, the salesperson is unable to advance the sale despite his or her efforts.

Frequent Stalls and Objections

As the salesperson attempts to move the sale forward, he or she is confronted with a never-ending series of barriers, stalls and objections. In essence, the prospect is signaling the salesperson to stop because what is being sold does not address their needs, wants, problems and concerns in a manner that he or she is interested in. Many of the older sales methods train salespeople to move forward and handle the objections until each has been resolved and the sale has been made. However, fewer buyers have the patience to play this game.

Remedies

Once in the mist of a sale, there are few alternatives to the salesperson other than starting over. Without a full understanding of the prospect's needs, the likelihood of a positive outcome is diminished.

Re-qualify the Prospect

In many instances it is necessary to completely start from the beginning to requalify the prospect to eliminate any faulty assumptions and misconceptions with hard data and facts. This includes determining if there is a legitimate and not a perceived need; the prospect's financial ability to make the purchase; the schedule timing of the purchase; realistic sales potential and who will make the buying decision and what criteria will be used. Decisions must be made if the prospect's business should be a priority and whether or not the salesperson should proceed or move on.

Reanalyze

Based upon the knowledge already gleaned during the sales process to this point, the salesperson will need to reanalyze the prospect's business using a series of probing questions that develop a comprehensive overview of the prospect's business and focuses on specific areas of concern.

Often prospects will answer questions using broad statements about their needs and levels of satisfaction with a current supplier. Often salespeople will accept these statements at face value without probing to uncover the specific details of what the prospect is talking about or their pain and discomfort with existing products or services.

There are a series of questions that salespeople can effective use to probe for needs and analyze a prospect's business:

History questions

– Identify optimal vs. actual conditions

Example: What have you used in the past? or What was your experience with ____?

Symptom questions

– Identify discontent

Example: Have you experienced any problems with ____?

Cause questions

– Define the problem

Example: What do you think the problem is with ____?

Complication questions

– Clarify the seriousness of the problem

Example: What does a problem like that cost you?

Cure questions

– Identify the prospect's expectation of value.

Example: What would a solution to that problem be worth to you?

After the probing questions have been asked, the salesperson will be able to design solutions around the buyer's needs. Successful buying solutions must be crafted around the essential features the prospect has specified as well as the secondary features they feel are important. The ideal solution will match the unique product features to the customer's specified needs. This approach creates a competitive advantage and effectively blocks the competition from getting the sale.

POINTS TO PONDER — SOMETHING TO THINK ABOUT

1. How have you recovered from a situation where the prospect was not qualified?
2. How thoroughly do you analyze your prospect's needs.

TRAINING ACTIVITY — APPLICATION & ACTION PLAN

Use the following categories to develop a series of questions (minimum of two for each) to probe a prospect's needs.

- History questions
- Symptom questions

- Cause questions
- Complication questions
- Cure questions

8

When to Walk Away

There is a point in the qualifying process when salespeople must make several critical decisions about a prospect that ultimately determines the direction that the sales relationship will take. These decisions shape the potential investment the salesperson intends to make in the prospect's business and determine their viability as a customer.

IMPLICATIONS — WHAT THIS MEANS TO YOU

Time management is an essential element for successful salespeople. In an ever-changing environment, salespeople must take the time to balance their responsibilities to existing customers with the need to develop and qualify new prospects.

Once the initial qualification process is completed, salespeople must make several critical decisions that go beyond whether a prospect will or will not buy a product. In between those choices there are a number of companies that don't fit either set of criteria. Salespeople must make decisions about these prospects since they may represent future sales potential for them. The optimal solution is to select the best prospects and work on them, but salespeople must look toward future growth and these prospects may require development and should be retained in the salesperson's pipeline.

STRATEGIES, TIPS & TECHNIQUES TO APPLY

The initial qualification process is a decision tree for salespeople to follow. Ideally, salespeople will have a pre-determined set of criteria that they can use to identify the best prospects to work on. This ideally provides them with a filter to comprehensively view a prospect's business. However, most salespeople are going to identify a number of companies that don't fit their criteria. These are the prospects that they must make several decisions about. Typically these decisions are going to fall into three categories:

Walk Away

The prospects that salespeople want to walk away from obviously have no possible potential of becoming customers. They typically have no need or use for a specific product or service or they have a need, but cannot afford to make a purchase.

There is a caveat to this category. This regards the prospect that cannot afford to make a purchase. In certain cases, the company is entirely too small and probably will never afford a product or service, however small companies do grow and the need and ability to buy might be present at a later date. Salespeople should be carefully not to offend these individuals since when they are in a position to buy they will remember how they were treated in the past.

Additionally, there are many companies impacted by budget problems that don't have the ability to buy now, but may be in the future. In these cases, salespeople might wish to place them in a pending category and check back from time to time to see if circumstances change.

Pending

Undoubtedly salespeople will come across prospects that are difficult to qualify because the buyer was uncooperative or refused to provide the information the salesperson needed to make a qualified decision. In these instances, the salesperson may have been unable to identify or contact someone with the buying authority or may have been brushed off because there was no initial interest.

Since insufficient information was developed, the salesperson is placed in limbo. Rather than waste time and resources, salespeople should place these prospects in a pending category and continue to work on them until they are able to get into the business and properly qualify it.

Reprioritize

There are prospects that require reexamination and may need to be reprioritized based upon potential sales volume, budgets, timing, application, or service demands. These prospects may have the potential to be excellent customers, but specific issues are preventing a salesperson from advancing the sale. The salesperson might need to plan to call on them when the timing of the sale is more advantageous and defer further action until there is a change in circumstances.

POINTS TO PONDER — SOMETHING TO THINK ABOUT

1. How do you make your qualifying decisions regarding specific types of prospects you encounter?
2. What defines a qualified prospect?

TRAINING ACTIVITY — APPLICATION & ACTION PLAN

1. Develop a system that allows you to efficiently make decisions about a prospect to determine whether they are worth the investment of your time and resources.
2. Identify the criteria and the various categories that each may fall into.
3. Determine the actions to be taken with each category.

About the Author

Timothy F. Bednarz, Ph.D. is CEO of the American Management Development Group, Inc. For over 20 years he has researched, designed and authored hundreds of learning and development programs used by Fortune 1000 companies.

He is also the author of *Great! What Makes Leaders Great. What They Did, How They Did It and What You Can Learn from It* (2011).

Speaking Availability

Timothy F. Bednarz, Ph.D. is available for speaking engagements for your next meeting or association event. He can be contacted at 800-654-4935 or by e-mail at timothy.bednarz@majorium.com.

Bulk Sales

Bulk sales of this book or any other titles available from Majorium Business Press. Inquiries can be directed to sales@majorium.com, or by phone at 800-6654-4935.

Quick Order Form

Fax orders: 715-342-1118. Send this form.

Telephone orders: Call 800-654-4935 toll-free. Have your credit card ready.

Email orders: sales@majorium.com

Postal orders: Majorium Business Press, 2025 Main Street, Stevens Point, WI 54481, USA.

Please send the following books:

____

____

____

____

Please send more FREE information on:

❑ Catalog ❑ Speaking/Seminars ❑ Mailing Lists ❑ Consulting

Name: __________________________________

Address: __________________________________

City: ____________________ State: _____ Zip: ________

Telephone: __________________________________

Email address: ______________________________

Sales tax: Please add 5.5% for products shipped to Wisconsin addresses.

Shipping by air:

United States: $4.00 for first book and $2.00 for each additional product.

International: $9.00 for first book; $5.00 for each additional product (estimate).

Made in United States
Cleveland, OH
05 November 2026

47675529R00030